The SaaS Psychology: Is Your Customer Frustrated, Ignoring, or Loving Your Product?

By Aries Ram

The information provided in this book is based on the author's experience, research, and observations in the field of SaaS product marketing and management. It is intended solely for educational and informational purposes. While every effort has been made to ensure accuracy, the author and publisher make no representations or warranties with respect to the completeness, reliability, or applicability of the content provided.

This book does not constitute professional advice, nor should it be relied upon as such. Readers are encouraged to seek appropriate professional guidance for their specific business, legal, or financial circumstances. The author and publisher disclaim any liability for any loss, risk, or damages, personal or otherwise, incurred directly or indirectly as a result of the use and application of any of the contents of this book.

All case studies, company references, and examples included in this book are either publicly available, adapted for educational purposes, or represent the author's interpretations. Unless explicitly stated, the author is not affiliated with, sponsored by, or endorsed by any of the companies mentioned.

The Voices That Shaped This Work

This book is not just my mind dump—it's the result of countless conversations, experiences, and insights shaped by the incredible people I've had the privilege to learn from.

First, to my clients and customers over the past decade: thank you. Every project, every feedback session, every late-night discussion about what's working (and what's not) gave me a front-row seat into how real people think, feel, and act when interacting with products. You've been my greatest teachers in understanding the psychology that makes SaaS succeed—or stumble.

To my readers—those who picked up my very first book, *The SaaS Prescription: Is Your Product a Painkiller, Antibiotic, or Vitamin?*

I owe you special gratitude. Your support, feedback, and motivation turned what started as an idea into a published work that found its way into your hands. The encouragement I received from you is what pushed me to write this second book, *The SaaS Psychology: Is Your Customer Frustrated, Ignoring, or Loving Your Product?*

And finally, to every SaaS founder, product manager, and marketer out there who dares to ask the hard questions about their product—you're the reason I write. Because when you win, your customers win, and I win too, on the flip side.

— **Aries Ram**

Table of Contents

Introduction: The Human Side of SaaS

This is my take: Most SaaS companies are super obsessed with features, pricing, lead conversion, CAC (customer acquisition cost), churn rate, and funnels.

But then one powerful lever is often ignored.

Yeah, you almost guessed it right!

It's the emotional connection between your product and your users.

You see, at the end of the day, your customers aren't some personas on spreadsheets or some data that deep research on ChatGPT gave you. They're real, sensible, or intelligent human beings—feeling, reacting, judging—every time they interact with your SaaS product.

Every click, every loading screen, every poorly worded error message triggers an emotion.

Sometimes it's an aha moment.

Sometimes it's frustration.

Most dangerously, sometimes it's disinterest.

And that emotional response?

It determines whether they'll stick with your product, recommend it, or silently churn.

Why User Psychology is the Ultimate Growth Hack

Think of it this way:

If your customer *loves* your product, no discount, competitor, or minor bug will push them away.

But if they're annoyed, confused, or emotionally detached, no amount of growth hacks or ad spend will save you.

Understanding **why** your users feel what they feel is the key to:

- Reducing churn.
- Boosting retention.
- Driving organic growth through advocacy.
- Building products people can't imagine living without.

Most growth tactics are temporary.

User psychology, however, compounds over time.

Is This Book For You & How To Use It?

This book is for you if you are a:

- **SaaS Founder** trying to build products that users truly care about.

- **Product Manager** aiming to create experiences that resonate emotionally.

- **Product Marketer** crafting positioning & messaging that connects with real human feelings.

It's not about fluffy theory.

It's about **practical psychology applied to SaaS** – diagnosing where your product stands emotionally with your users, and giving you proven playbooks to shift frustration into love.

You'll learn:

- How to recognize the emotional signals your users are sending.
- How to diagnose whether your product is frustrating, ignored, or loved.
- How to strategically shift customer emotions to drive growth.

Use this book as a **field guide**.
Read it cover to cover for the full picture, or jump into the sections most relevant to your current challenges.

Because once you master SaaS Psychology, you'll never look at user feedback, product decisions, or growth metrics the same way again.

Part 1: The Psychology of SaaS Users

Chapter 1: The Emotional Spectrum of SaaS Users

You've poured your heart into building that feature, rewritten your onboarding twice, and A/B-tested your pricing page until your eyes blurred. Yet when you log in to your dashboard at 8 a.m., the numbers haven't moved. Why?

Because behind every metric, every click, and every churned account is a human—their feelings guiding their decisions far more than logic ever could. In this chapter, we'll map out the three emotional zones every SaaS user inhabits—Frustration, Indifference, and Love—and show you precisely how those feelings translate into behavior and business results.

Frustration, Ignorance, Love: The 3 Emotional Zones

1. Frustration Zone

Imagine Sarah, a busy marketing manager. She signs up for your tool, hoping to save hours on campaign reporting. Instead, she finds convoluted menus, jargon-filled tooltips, and—worst of all—an onboarding flow that stops midway with a cryptic "Unknown error."

Her feelings?

Anger, **overwhelm**, **betrayal**.

Frustration is the loudest alarm bell your product can ring. It drives immediate churn, support tickets, and negative word-of-mouth. One frustrated user might broadcast their pain across LinkedIn or to your competitor's sales team. In metric terms, frustration looks like:

- Spike in support requests within the first 48 hours
- Low completion rates on critical tasks (eg, "Upload your first file")
- A surge in "I give up" cancellations

Key takeaway: Frustration demands **immediate** action. Hunt down the error messages, the dead-end workflows, the slow-loading screens. Every millisecond saved, every ambiguous message clarified, is a step closer to turning that fury into calm curiosity.

2. Ignorance Zone

Next, meet Alex, a product manager who hears about your app through a blog post. He signs up, pokes around for a few days, but never really “wows” his team. There are no bug reports, no raves, but also no memorable “aha!” moments. He simply... stops logging in.

His feelings?

Boredom, neutrality, meh.

Ignorance is the silent killer. It doesn’t look as dramatic as rage-quit frustration, but it kills growth just as effectively. Indifferent users drift away without raising alarms, leaving you wondering, “What happened?” Key ignorance signals include:

- Users who log in fewer than once a week after the first month
- Feature adoption rates stuck at single digits
- High “dormant user” segments in your cohort analysis

Key takeaway: Rescue indifference with **relevance** and **personalization**. Cultivate emotional relevance through targeted in-product nudges, timely check-ins, and contextual tips that solve *their* real problems. Make them feel seen.

3. Love Zone

Finally, picture Priya, a small-business founder. From the moment she first uses your drag-and-drop dashboard, she's hooked. She tells a colleague, and they join too. She tweets a tip. She voluntarily records a testimonial video.

Her feelings? **Delight**, **trust**, **advocacy**.

Love is the holy grail. These users defend you when bugs slip through, forgive pricing changes, and bring in new customers effortlessly. The metrics of love are:

- Net Promoter Score (NPS) consistently above 60
- A viral coefficient >1 (every user brings in more than one new user)
- High lifetime value (LTV) even as price increases

Key takeaway: Cultivate love by weaving **delight** into every interaction—micro-animations that reward completion, surprise "thank you" notes after milestones, and community features that let superfans connect.

How Emotions Drive Behavior & Business Outcomes

It's tempting to think of SaaS growth purely as a numbers game: increase trial sign-ups, optimize conversion, lower churn by a percentage point. But those percentages are **symptoms**, not root causes. They're reflections of your users' felt experiences.

- **Emotional friction** (frustration) inflates support costs, spikes churn, and poisons your brand reputation.
- **Emotional detachment** (indifference) silently drifts users out of your funnel, flattening growth and hiding warning signs until it's too late.
- **Emotional resonance** (love) compounds over time, turning users into evangelists and making every marketing dollar more effective.

By learning to **read** these emotional signals in your data—chat transcripts, usage patterns, survey feedback—you can move beyond reactive fixes into proactive design. You'll know **before** a major churn wave hits that frustration is spiking; you'll spot the growing segment of indifferent users steered toward the exit; and you'll identify features your power users love so you can double down.

Looking Ahead

Understanding these three emotional zones isn't a one-and-done checklist. It's a continuous practice: every product decision, every marketing message, every support response either pushes a user closer to frustration or indifference—or pulls them deeper into love.

In the next chapter, we'll dive into **Cognitive Load & UX**, exploring exactly how simplicity (or lack thereof) sets the emotional stage for every user interaction. You'll learn concrete frameworks to eliminate overwhelm, guide users effortlessly, and build the confidence that keeps them coming back.

Let's keep turning friction into flow—and turning users into lifelong fans.

Chapter 2: Cognitive Load & UX — Why Simplicity Wins

You've just signed up for a new SaaS tool that promises to "revolutionize your workflow."

Excited, you click through screens full of buttons, drop-downs, and jargon.

Five minutes in, you're lost.

Ten minutes later, you're off to find a simpler alternative.

This scenario happens more often than you think. Every extra menu, every unclear label, and every undocumented feature adds to your user's **cognitive load**—the mental effort they expend to understand and use your product.

When that load becomes too heavy, adoption grinds to a halt.

How Overwhelm Kills Adoption

1. **Decision Paralysis**

    ○ Presenting too many choices at once, and your user freezes.

    ○ Example: A dashboard with dozens of widgets might look powerful—but to a first-time user, it's a puzzle box.

    ○ Impact: Low feature discoverability and skyrocketing bounce rates.

2. **Hidden Costs of Complexity**

    ○ Every new button carries an unspoken question: "What happens if I click this?"

    ○ Uncertainty creates friction. Users will abandon tasks rather than risk a wrong move.

    ○ Impact: Abandoned sign-up flows, unfilled profiles, and "I'll do it later" bookmark folders that never get revisited.

3. **Support Overload**
   - Complex interfaces generate more "How do I...?" tickets.
   - Your support team becomes a fire brigade, patching up user confusion instead of proactively delighting customers.
   - Impact: Rising support costs, longer response times, and frustrated users venting publicly.

Designing for Intuitive Action, Not User Manuals

Your job as a product designer or PM isn't to cram every capability into a 100-page manual.

It's to guide users—step by step—with as little mental effort as possible.

1. **Embrace Progressive Disclosure**
   - Reveal options only when they become relevant.
   - Show the basic "innocent" interface to new users, and unlock advanced features as they gain confidence.
   - Benefit: Users never feel lost in a sea of controls.
2. **Use Clear, Action-Oriented Labels**
   - Replace generic button text ("Submit," "Next") with task-specific verbs ("Generate Report," "Invite Your Team").
   - Benefit: Users immediately know the outcome of every click.

3. **Leverage Visual Affordances**

    - Design buttons to look pressable, fields to look editable, and warnings to look urgent.
    - Use whitespace strategically to group related elements.
    - Benefit: Your interface communicates its own rules—no manual required.

4. **Micro-Interactions & Feedback**

    - Show progress bars, animated checkmarks, or subtle hover states.
    - Immediate feedback reassures users they're on the right track.
    - Benefit: Reduces anxiety and reinforces momentum.

5. **Pattern Consistency**

    - Use common conventions (hamburger menus, card layouts, toggle switches) rather than inventing new paradigms.

    - Benefit: Users bring existing mental models, slashing the learning curve.

A Would-Be Real-World Example

Consider a popular project-management app that replaced its sprawling sidebar (20+ links) with a two-tab design: "Projects" and "Tasks." Hidden behind an "Advanced" toggle were reporting and analytics tools—features only power users needed. Overnight, first-time activation rates jumped by 30%, and support tickets about navigation dropped by half.

Your Key Takeaways

- **Every extra decision is a barrier.** Strip your interface down to the essentials.

- **Guide don't instruct.** Let your design teach through its own patterns and feedback.

- **Delight in the details.** Micro-interactions aren't frivolous—they build confidence and habit.

By intentionally reducing cognitive load, you transform frustration into focus—and transform first-time users into power users.

In the next chapter, we'll explore **The Trust Factor**: how to build confidence in every click, and why trust is the bedrock of lasting customer relationships.

Chapter 3: The Trust Factor – Building Confidence in Every Click

My POV - "Your Customers aren't just People who buy from you—but also the People who decide if you should exist".

Now this is important, just take 7 minutes off this book!

Think back to the last time you hesitated before clicking a button in a new app.

Was it a "Delete Account" link?

A "Buy Now" button?

That tiny flicker of doubt—"What happens if I do this?"—is the enemy of adoption.

In SaaS, **trust** is your secret weapon. Every trust signal you embed is a tiny deposit in your users' confidence bank. Withdraw too much doubt, and they'll abandon ship.

Let's explore how to craft an experience that feels as safe as it is empowering.

Reducing anxiety with trust signals.

Anxiety Is the Hidden Churn Driver

Anxiety shows up as hesitation—users second-guessing every click, hovering over a link for seconds that feel like minutes, or giving up altogether. When you can't predict the outcome of an action, your brain treats it like a potential threat. That threat triggers:

- **Fear of making a mistake** ("Will I lose my data?")
- **Fear of regret** ("What if I choose the wrong pricing tier?")
- **Fear of complexity** ("This seems harder than I thought.")

Even if your product delivers immense value, these tiny fears add up to **churn**.

Your mission: **reduce uncertainty** at every step.

Embed Trust Signals Everywhere

Trust signals are cues that ease anxiety by promising safety, clarity, or social proof. They needn't be flashy; subtle is best.

- **Security Badges & Encryption Notices**
  • Display "256-bit encryption" or "SOC 2 compliant" near password fields or billing forms.
  • A small lock icon next to sensitive inputs reassures users that their data is guarded.

- **Friendly Progress Indicators**
  • "Step 2 of 4" is better than "Next." It tells users exactly where they are—and how much is left.
  • Visual progress bars or checkmarks reward forward motion and squash the dread of endless forms.

- **Clear Ownership of Errors**
  • If something goes wrong, own it: "Oops! We hit a snag saving your report. Let's try again."
  • Human-tone error messages ("Looks like that username's taken. Want to try another?") feel collaborative, not punitive.

- **Social Proof & Testimonials**
  • "Trusted by 10,000+ marketing teams" on your signup

page nudges indecisive visitors.
• Short quotes or logos of well-known customers build credibility without interrupting the flow.

- **Inline Help & Tooltips**
  • Contextual, hover-activated tips ("What's a webhook?") prevent users from leaving the page to search for answers.
  • Embed a "?" icon next to jargon—no heavy-handed pop-up manuals required.

Onboarding Flows That Make Users Feel Smart

A stellar onboarding does more than teach; it **celebrates** every small win, creating a feeling of mastery that fuels further exploration.

1. **Ask Only What You Need**

    - Resist the temptation to collect every data point upfront. Each extra field is a mental tax.

    - **Example:** Rather than "What industry are you in? What's your team size? What's your budget?"

ask one critical question now and defer the rest until you can demonstrate value.

2. **Show Value Before You Ask for Effort**

    - Let users experience a "wow" moment within the first 3 clicks.

    - **Example:** A payment-processing tool could immediately show "You've just created your first payment link! Here's how to share it."

3. **Use Milestones & Micro-Rewards**

    - Celebrate small achievements: "Nice work! You've invited your first teammate."

    - Animate a confetti burst or progress badge—these dopamine hits build confidence.

4. **Personalize the Journey**

    - Leverage the one piece of information you asked: "Welcome, Priya! Ready to streamline your 3-

person team?"

    - Tailored welcome messages show you see them as individuals, not just email addresses.

5. **Offer Guided Tours, But Let Users Skip**

    - A short, skippable tutorial caters to both new users and power users.

    - **Tip:** Include a "Show me around" link in the header for later, so explorers can self-serve guidance on their own timeline.

Putting Trust & Confidence into Practice

Imagine a user signing up for your CRM:

1. **Signup Page:** They see "Trusted by 20,000+ sales teams" under the email field.

2. **Password Field:** A small lock icon and "256-bit encryption" note appear.

3. **Onboarding Step 1:** “Hi Alex, let’s add your first contact. You’ll see tracking insights immediately.”

4. **Action Taken:** A confetti animation celebrates the new contact.

5. **Next Step:** “Great! Now invite a teammate or skip ahead to explore deals.”

Each step is **clear**, **rewarding**, and **reduces doubt**. Users don’t wonder what happens next—they feel equipped to explore.

Key Takeaways

- **Anxiety costs customers** before they ever invite a teammate or enter a payment method.
- **Trust signals**—from security badges to social proof—act like handrails on a steep staircase.
- **Onboarding that feels like a conversation** makes users feel capable, not overwhelmed.

When you build confidence into every interaction, you don't just reduce churn—you breed champions.

In the next chapter, we'll unlock the secrets of **Habits, Hooked Models & Retention Psychology** so that you can turn those champions into lifelong power users.

Chapter 4: Habits, Hooked Models & Retention Psychology

Again, my POV - **"Growth grabs attention. Retention earns devotion. If you're not habit-forming, you're forgettable**."

Anyone can get a user to sign up once. That's not the hard part. The real challenge—and the real money—is in getting them to **come back**.

Again and again.

Without needing a nudge, a discount, or a desperate reminder email.

Retention is what separates a product that *sparkles* from one that *sticks*.

It's what separates apps that trend for a month from those that turn into verbs. ("Google it." "Slack me." "Zoom in.")

And behind every sticky SaaS product is the same secret: it doesn't just solve a problem.

It becomes a **habit**.

Let's unpack the psychology of stickiness—and how you can build it into your product from day one.

The Science of Habit-Forming Products

Habits aren't born overnight. They're built through a loop—a psychological cycle that rewards action and makes it easier to repeat.

In his book *Hooked*, Nir Eyal lays out a model used by many habit-forming products. Here's how it works in a SaaS context:

The Hook Model:

1. **Trigger** – The cue that initiates the behavior.

    - **External Trigger**: Email alert, Slack message, push notification.

    - **Internal Trigger**: Boredom, anxiety, pressure to perform—emotional states that drive users to seek relief or control.

2. **Action** – The behavior the user performs in anticipation of a reward.

    - Posting a task. Sending a message. Checking a dashboard.

3. **Variable Reward** – A satisfying, often unpredictable outcome.

    - Seeing new analytics. Receiving feedback. Watching progress grow.

4. **Investment** – The user does something to increase their likelihood of returning.

    - Uploads files. Invites teammates. Personalizes settings.

Every pass through the loop tightens the user's connection to your product. The more they invest, the harder it becomes to leave.

When & How to Build Stickiness

You don't need to gamify everything or add "likes" and "badges" to make your SaaS product sticky.

You just need to align with the *real-world motivations* of your users and reduce the friction between need and reward.

Here's how:

a) Find the Frequency Sweet Spot

Ask yourself: *How often should a successful user interact with my product?*

- A CRM might be used daily.
- An SEO audit tool might be used weekly.
- A budget forecasting platform might only need monthly check-ins.

The key is **not to force unnecessary usage**, but to design around **natural frequency**. Once you identify it, build lightweight loops that keep users coming back at just the right moments.

💡 *To me, stickiness isn't about more time in the app. It's about becoming part of the user's workflow.*

b) Design with 'Return Hooks' in Mind

Your user should always have a reason to return that's tied to *value*—not vanity.

Instead of:

- ➔ "We miss you!"

Try:

- ★ "3 new insights on your latest campaign"
- ★ "Your sales pipeline needs follow-up on 4 deals"

Value-based return triggers build trust and justify attention.

c) Make Progress Visible and Addictive

People are hardwired to chase progress. Give them momentum they can see and feel.

- Progress bars for setup or onboarding
- Streaks or milestones for repeated actions
- Visual dashboards that improve with activity

Example:
A project management tool that shows "You're 80% closer to shipping this sprint" can drive re-engagement better than a generic reminder.

d) Let Users Invest in Your Product

The more users *personalize, upload, build, or invite*, the deeper their psychological investment.

Let's say you run a document collaboration SaaS. If your user:

- Creates a folder structure
- Uploads client decks
- Tags a teammate

They're not just using your product—they're *building* in it. And people don't walk away from things they've built.

Retention Isn't One Feature. It's a Feeling.

Retention doesn't hinge on one magic feature. It's the *emotional residue* your product leaves behind.

Ask yourself:

- **Does my product feel like progress?**
- **Do users feel smarter, faster, and more in control after using it?**
- **If they skipped a day, would they notice? Miss it? Crave it?**

If the answer is yes, you're not just solving problems—you're changing behavior. That's retention gold.

Key Takeaways

- Habit-forming products are built on **triggers**, **actions**, **variable rewards**, and **user investment**.

- Stickiness isn't about forcing engagement—it's about being useful when users need you most.

- Retention grows when users **feel progress**, **see results**, and **invest effort** into the product.

- The best SaaS products become invisible: not because users forget them, but because they can't imagine work without them.

In the next chapter, we'll dive into **Emotional Analytics**—because numbers alone don't tell you how users *feel*, and that feeling is often the real reason they stay... or leave.

Part 2: Diagnosing Your Product's Emotional Impact

Chapter 5: Is Your Product Frustrating Users?

My POV boss **"Users won't always tell you they're frustrated. They'll just disappear."**

You've been there.

You launch a new feature.

You announce it with pride.

And then... silence.

Or worse, support tickets.

Or even worse—uninstalls.

Frustration isn't always loud.

Most of the time, it's a silent churn.

A blank stare.

A closed tab.

But when users are frustrated, they leave clues.

And if you know what to look for, you can fix the friction before it becomes fatal.

Let's explore how to detect frustration—before it drives your users away—and how to fix the most common product sins behind it.

Some Symptoms, Warning Signs & Data Cues

Your product may be shipping features, but are users shipping out? Here are the key signals that frustration is brewing under the surface:

a) Behavioral Drop-Offs

- Users sign up but never activate.
- Users complete onboarding but never return.
- Frequent visits with low engagement (lots of clicks, little progress).

Data Cue: High drop-off rates after the first or second session. Check your funnel analytics—where are users bailing?

b) Support Ticket Patterns

- Repetitive questions: "How do I do X?" means X isn't obvious.
- Angry language: Frustration often shows in tone before exit.

Data Cue: Tag and categorize your tickets. Look for volume spikes around certain features or pages.

c) Rage Clicks & Dead Ends

- Users clicking the same button repeatedly = unmet expectations.
- Pages that end with "What now?" = confusion creates psychological dead zones.

Data Cue: Use session replay tools (like Hotjar, FullStory) to catch these moments of friction in action.

d) Abandoned Flows

- Unfinished forms, skipped steps, or half-filled profiles are signs of complexity overload.

Data Cue: Drop-off analytics within core workflows reveal where effort outweighs perceived value.

My Favourite #5 Common Product Sins & How to Fix Them

If your users are frustrated, odds are your product is committing one (or more) of these cardinal sins:

Sin #1: Complexity Without Clarity

"It's powerful" is not an excuse for "It's confusing."

- **Fix:** Use plain language. Replace jargon with context. Write labels like you're explaining it to a smart friend who's never seen it before.

Sin #2: Forcing Users to Think Too Much

Cognitive load is the silent killer of adoption.

- **Fix:** Break big tasks into smaller, digestible steps. Use visual hierarchy—bold what matters, fade what doesn't. Reduce the number of decisions per screen.

Sin #3: No Feedback = No Confidence

Clicking a button and seeing nothing? That's a trust-breaker.

- **Fix:** Micro-interactions matter. Add loaders, animations, checkmarks—anything to say, "Yes, your action worked."

Sin #4: Over-Onboarding or Under-Onboarding

Too much information, or not enough context, is both deadly.

- **Fix:** Offer just-in-time help, not just a linear tutorial. Use empty states to guide users gently into the experience.

Sin #5: Lack of Emotional UX

Your product may work, but how does it make users *feel*?

- **Fix:** Humanize your microcopy. Celebrate small wins. Apologize like a person, not a machine. UX is emotional—design for reassurance, not just resolution.

From Frustration to Flow

Every source of friction is an opportunity to build love. Frustration isn't failure—it's feedback in disguise. The more you study it, the more power you gain to transform user tension into trust.

The SaaS products users love aren't perfect. They're just responsive. Empathetic. They listen, they adapt, and they remove obstacles before the user even sees them.

Key takeaway: If you want loyalty, reduce friction. If you want love, reduce frustration.

In the next chapter, we'll explore how **indifference**—not frustration—is often the *real* reason users ghost your product.

And what to do about it.

Chapter 6: The Silent Killer – Indifference & Ignored Products

My POV - **"Users who complain still care. The ones you need to worry about are the ones who go quiet."**

If frustration is loud, indifference is deadly silence.

You can recover from an angry user.

You can improve a buggy feature.

But when users stop caring — when they quietly drift away and never look back — that's when your product is in real trouble.

Let's get brutally honest: most SaaS products don't die from hate. They die from being ignored.

Why Being Ignored Is Worse Than Being Hated

When someone hates your product, they're still emotionally engaged. There's still a relationship — even if it's strained.

But indifference?

It's the void.

You're not useful.

You're not annoying.

You're just... nothing.

An angry user still has hope. An indifferent user has moved on.

Indifference or ignoring is more dangerous than bugs or bad UX. It's what happens when your product fails to earn a place in your user's mind, workflow, or day.

And here's the kicker: most teams don't even know it's happening — until the churn reports show up too late.

Emotional Disengagement Metrics to Track

To fight indifference, you have to measure emotional engagement, not just activity.

Here's how to spot users slipping away:

1) Time-to-First-Value (TTFV) Is Too Long

If it takes too long for users to experience the value of your product, they won't stick around.

- **Fix it:** Shorten onboarding. Show results faster. Focus on the *first win*.

2) Feature Abandonment

Do users try a feature once and never touch it again? That's a red flag.

- **Fix it:** Reframe the benefit. Educate through tooltips, nudges, or "Did you know?" moments.

3) No Support Tickets

Sounds like a good thing? It's not — if your users aren't asking questions, they're not using the product.

- **Fix it:** Re-engage with in-app messages or emails asking, "How can we help you get more out of [Product]?"

4) Inactive, But Still Paying

These are the silent churners – the people who forgot they even subscribed.

- **Fix it:** Trigger win-back campaigns. Offer a guided tour, or even a conversation: "Haven't seen you in a while – can we help?"

5) Flat Session Heatmaps

If session replays show people staring at the screen without action, that's disengagement in motion.

- **Fix it:** Guide users with clearer next steps, nudges, and smart defaults.

How to Reignite User Interest

You can't demand attention. You earn it – through relevance, emotion, and timing.

a) Show Value in Their Language

Don't list features. Show what outcomes they get. Make it about *them*.

- Instead of: "New analytics dashboard."
- Say: "Spot trends faster and make smarter decisions — in one view."

b) Personalize the Experience

Generic equals forgettable. Use their name, role, and past behavior. Make them feel known.

c) Create Small Moments of Delight

Micro-wins. Progress bars. Celebratory copy. Emotional UX makes people feel something — and that's what makes them come back.

d) Remind Them of the Before & After

Help users remember what life was like before your product. Help them *feel* the improvement.

"Before [*Your Tool*], it took 3 hours. Now it takes 12 minutes. That's your time back."

A Quick Thought: Don't Settle for Passive Users

In SaaS, indifference is often disguised as "quiet customers." But quiet isn't calm — it's the calm before the churn.

So don't just ask, "Are users active?"

Ask: **"Do users care?"**

Because if they don't — they won't stay.

Chapter 7: From Like to Love — Signs Your Product Is Winning Hearts

Another POV of mine on which you can write a short content on LinkedIn - "**When your product moves from liked to loved, you stop selling — you start celebrating.**"

You've fixed the bugs, smoothed the UX wrinkles, and quelled the silence of indifference.

Now it's time to recognize the magic moments when your users don't just use your product... they *champion* it.

True product love is precious, rare, and wildly powerful.

Let's explore how to spot it — and then fan those flames until your customers become your greatest growth engine.

Indicators of True Product Love

a) Organic Referrals

When users tell their friends, colleagues, or communities about your product — without you asking — you've earned advocacy. Listen for:

- Mentions on social media threads
- "Have you tried X?" conversations over coffee
- Referral spikes with no new marketing spend

b) Community Engagement

Lovers of your product don't just consume; they contribute. They post in your forums, answer newcomers' questions, and create content. Watch for:

- User-generated tutorials, templates, or plug-ins
- High activity in customer groups or Slack channels
- Peer-to-peer helps reduce your support load

c) High Net Promoter Scores (NPS)

An NPS above 50 is great. Above 70? That's love territory. But go deeper than the number:

- Read the verbatim feedback for emotional words: "game-changer," "life-saving," "I can't imagine..."

- Track sentiment over time to see if love is growing or waning

d) Feature Wishlist Alignment

Your power users don't just submit random ideas — they request enhancements that match your roadmap vision. That alignment means they're invested in *your* journey, not just their own.

e) Premium Tier Conversion

When free-trial users or low-tier subscribers upgrade without discount prompts, they're voting with their wallets because they genuinely value the extra power you provide.

How to Amplify Positive Emotional Triggers

Once you see love budding, water it generously. Here's how:

a. Celebrate Milestones Together

- Send a quick note: "Congrats on hitting 100 tasks completed!"
- Roll out virtual badges or a public leaderboard for top contributors.
- Host "Customer Appreciation" webinars where you spotlight stories from your most passionate users.

b. Deepen Personal Connections

- Invite top fans to a private beta or feedback roundtable.
- Offer "insider" status with sneak peeks at upcoming features.
- Hand-write (or personalize) thank-you emails when they renew or upgrade.

c. Empower Them to Shine

- Create a "Customer Spotlight" blog series or newsletter feature.
- Provide co-branding assets so they can showcase how they use your product.
- Offer affiliate or ambassador programs that reward them for sharing their success.

d. Layer in Delightful Surprises

- Randomly send a small gift card or swag to users who've hit major usage milestones.
- Embed Easter eggs — a hidden animation or personalized greeting — when they accomplish something great.
- Drop unexpected "thank you" messages in the app after a streak of consistent usage.

e. Make Their Feedback Come to Life

- Publicly credit users when you ship a feature they inspired.

- Keep a "You Asked, We Listened" section in your release notes.

- Celebrate each user's role in your roadmap—because when love is mutual, users feel ownership over your product's future.

Key Takeaways

- **True product love shows up** in organic referrals, community contributions, enthusiastic feedback, and self-initiated upgrades.

- **Amplify emotional triggers** by celebrating wins, deepening connections, empowering user stories, delighting with surprises, and honoring feedback.

- **When users love you, they don't just stay—** they bring others, defend you in the face of bugs, and invest in your shared future.

You've now learned to recognize love and stoke its fires.

In the next section, **Part 3**, we'll dive into strategic playbooks—step-by-step recipes for rescuing frustration, igniting interest, and cultivating evangelists at scale.

Let's keep that love burning bright.

Part 3: Strategy Playbooks to Shift Customer Emotions

Chapter 8: Frustrated to Engaged — The Rescue Playbook

"Frustration is a cry for help. Your mission: answer it before they hit the exit button."

Even the best products hit a rough patch. A confusing new feature, a lagging server, an onboarding form that trips up 20% of your users—each issue breeds frustration.

But frustration isn't fatal if you have a rescue plan.

In this chapter, I'll arm you with UX quick wins, and a support & communication framework to rebuild trust—and re-engage users—fast.

UX Quick Wins: Patch Friction Holes Fast

1. **One-Click Undo**

    - Mistakes happen. Give users a clear, visible "Undo" or "Revert" action after any destructive operation.

- **Impact:** Reduces fear of exploration and keeps users clicking with confidence.

2. **Inline Validation & Guidance**

    - Don't make users submit a form to learn they missed a field. Validate as they type, and show tips in context.

    - **Impact:** Cuts form-related support tickets by half and speeds task completion.

3. **Simplify Critical Flows**

    - Audit your top 3 tasks (e.g., "Create report," "Invite teammate," "Process payment"). Strip every unnecessary step or field.

    - **Impact:** Faster time-to-value; fewer drop-offs in essential workflows.

4. **Speed & Feedback**

    - Even a 200-ms spinner feels faster than a frozen screen. Use skeleton loaders or subtle animations to show progress.

- **Impact:** Lowers perceived wait times and prevents rage clicks.

5. **Visual Hierarchy Reset**

    - Spotlight the primary action with bold colors and whitespace. Demote secondary or risky buttons (like "Delete") into menus or smaller styles.

    - **Impact:** Guides the eye, reduces accidental clicks, and clarifies next steps.

Support, Communication & Expectation Management

A. Proactive Outreach

- **Automated Friction Alerts**

    - Set up monitoring to flag users stalled in key flows for >3 minutes or who hit repeated errors.

    - Trigger an in-app message or email: "Need help getting past [step]? Click here to chat with our team."

- **On-Demand Office Hours**
    - Offer weekly "drop-in" Zoom sessions for new users to ask questions live.
    - Promote these as a value-add, not a sales pitch.

B. Empathetic Support

- **Tone Over Templates**
    - Train your support team to lead with empathy: "I'm sorry you ran into this—we'll fix it right now."
    - Personalize responses with the user's name and specific context instead of canned replies.
- **Fast, Transparent Resolution**

- Even if you don't have an immediate fix, acknowledge the issue and share your next steps:

    1. We're investigating.

    2. We'll update you by [time].

    3. Here's a temporary workaround.

C. Reset Expectations

- **Feature Roadmap Visibility**

    - Maintain a public roadmap (a simple Trello or Notion board) and link to it when users ask, "When will you fix X?"

    - Allow users to upvote issues so they feel heard and prioritized.

- **Release Notes That Celebrate Fixes**

    - In every monthly update, highlight "You Spoke, We Listened" fixes first. Use friendly language:

"You told us creating a new dashboard was clunky. Now it's one click."

Putting the Rescue Playbook into Action

1. **Audit Your Pain Points:** Run a quick "frustration sprint" to identify your top three blockers.

2. **Deploy UX Patches:** Implement at least two quick-win edits this week.

3. **Stand Up Your Support Cadence:** Launch one proactive touchpoint (in-app ping or office hour) within 48 hours.

4. **Communicate Transparently:** Share progress openly and celebrate fixes with your users.

By moving swiftly to resolve pain and communicate with genuine care, you'll convert frustrated users into engaged advocates—and protect your growth from the silent threat of churn.

Ready to tackle **Chapter 9: Indifferent to Interested — The Activation Playbook** next?

Let me know, and we'll keep this momentum rolling.

Chapter 9: Indifferent to Interested – The Activation Playbook

"Indifference is a window closing—but activation is that first spark that reopens it."

When your users have gone quiet—no support tickets, no rage clicks, no love notes—it's easy to assume they're just fine. But silence often masks a deeper truth: **they don't care**.

And when they don't care, they slip closer to the exit.

The Activation Playbook is your toolkit for reigniting curiosity, delivering timely relevance, and moving users from "*meh*" to "*let's see what this can do*."

In this chapter, you'll discover:

(1) High-Impact Re-Engagement Campaigns

Re-engagement isn't begging users to come back—it's offering them a reason they can't ignore.

A. The Personal Check-In

- **Why it works**: A simple, human touch reminds users there's a real team behind the product.
- **What to send**: "Hey [Name], noticed you haven't used [Product] in a bit. Stuck on anything? Let us help."
- **Timing tip**: Trigger after 7 days of inactivity for daily tools, or after 30 days for monthly tools.

B. 'What You're Missing' Insights

- **Why it works**: People fear missing out on progress or opportunity.
- **What to send**: "Since you last logged in, your team created 15 new tasks. Jump back in to see wherc they landed!"
- **Data required**: Activity logs, feature usage summaries.

C. Outcome-Focused Drip Sequences

- **Why it works**: A series of targeted emails or in-app messages can guide users through small wins.
- **Structure**:

1. Email 1: Quick tip + link to one-click action. (e.g., "Export your first report.")
2. Email 2 (Day 3): Customer success story + CTA. ("See how [Company] cut time by 40%.")
3. Email 3 (Day 7): Limited-time offer or bonus content. ("Get a free 1-on-1 template review.")

- **Key**: Keep them short, visual, and centered on user benefits.

D. In-App Nudges & Banners

- **Why it works**: Timing is everything. Catch users in the moment, when they're most receptive.
- **Examples**:
    - **A banner**: "Did you know you can integrate with Slack? Enable it now."
    - **A modal**: "Need a refresher? Watch this 60-second tutorial."

(2) Building Emotional Relevance with Messaging & Positioning

You've got their attention—now make them feel seen.

A. Speak Their Language

- **Pain point framing**: Replace generic "boost productivity" with "stop juggling spreadsheets at midnight."
- **Empathy statements**: "We know how overwhelming it is to manage X—here's how we can help."

B. Spotlight Their Identity

- **Role-based messaging**: "For busy marketing leads" vs. "For solo entrepreneurs."
- **Use cases that mirror their world**: "Imagine launching campaigns in 10 minutes."

C. Leverage Social Proof Strategically

- **Peer testimonials**: "Our head of growth at [Similar Company] loves this feature."
- **Quantifiable results**: "Save 2 hours per week—just like 85% of our users did."

D. Create a Narrative Arc

- **Before ➔ After**: Paint a picture of life before your solution and the transformation it delivers.
- **Micro-stories**: Tiny anecdotes or quotes that humanize the experience.

E. Use Emotional Triggers in CTAs

- **Curiosity**: "See the report your boss will ask for."
- **Belonging**: "Join 5,000+ teams already simplifying workflows."
- **Urgency** (sparingly): "Try this feature before your trial ends."

Putting Activation into Practice

1. **Audit Inactive Cohorts:** Identify users with zero or minimal engagement in the last 'X' period.
2. **Choose 1-2 Campaigns:** Start with the Personal Check-In and '*What You're Missing*' insights.
3. **Draft Messages:** Write copy that zeroes in on one clear action and emotional benefit.
4. **Measure & Iterate:** Track open rates, click-through rates, and reactivation metrics. Refine messaging weekly.

By combining smart data triggers with heartfelt messaging, you'll turn silence into curiosity—and indifference into action.

In the next chapter, we'll explore **Chapter 10: From Like to Love — The Evangelism Playbook**, where we'll turn those activated users into vocal advocates.

Chapter 10: From Like to Love — The *Evangelism* Playbook

"Advocates don't just use your product—they make it part of their story."

You've guided users from frustration to flow, reawakened the indifferent, and activated curiosity.

Now comes the pinnacle: turning satisfied customers into ***evangelists***—the passionate voices who share your product because they *believe* in it.

Evangelism isn't accidental.

It's engineered through emotional loyalty programs, vibrant communities, and feedback loops that honor your users' voices.

Let's map out how to build a movement, not just a user base.

Turning Users into Advocates

Advocates are your unpaid salesforce. They bring credibility, authenticity, and trust—qualities no ad budget can buy.

A. Make Advocacy Easy

- **Single-click referrals:** Embed "Invite a friend" or "Share this report" buttons in the product. Keep friction to zero.
- **Pre-written templates:** Provide email or social media snippets users can customize and share.

B. Reward Genuine Supporters

- **Tiered ambassador programs:** Recognize top referrers with exclusive perks—early feature access, swag, or public shout-outs.
- **Point & badge systems:** Let users earn points for every share, testimonial, or resource they create.

C. Celebrate Their Wins

- Feature customer success stories on your blog or social channels.
- Host "Advocate Spotlight" posts where you interview top champions.
- Make them feel like heroes—because they are.

Emotional Loyalty Programs

Loyalty goes beyond discounts. It's about creating emotional bonds that fuel long-term devotion.

A. Purpose-Driven Rewards

- Align rewards with your users' values: donate to charity for every referral, or plant a tree for each milestone.
- Show impact: "Together, we've planted 500 trees in our community."

B. Experiential Benefits

- Invite loyal users to VIP events, webinars with founders, or backstage product sneak peeks.
- Offer co-creation sessions where they influence feature development.

C. Surprise & Delight

- Unexpectedly upgrade their plan for a month.
- Send personalized thank-you notes or small gifts for renewal anniversaries.

Building Community & Feedback Loops

A thriving community transforms users into collaborators—and that collaboration breeds ownership and advocacy.

(A) Cultivate Safe, Accessible Spaces

- Launch a dedicated Slack, Discord, or forum for your product users.
- Set clear guidelines to foster respectful, inclusive dialogue.

(B) Facilitate Peer-to-Peer Support

- Encourage users to answer one another's questions.
- Highlight stellar community answers in your official documentation.

(C) Better Co-Create with Your Users

- Regularly solicit feedback via surveys, polls, and feature-vote boards.
- Run quarterly "Product Council" sessions where top users preview and critique roadmap items.

(D) Close the Loop Publicly

- When you ship a feature requested by the community, announce: "You asked, we listened."
- Tag or thank the users who influenced the decision.

Key Takeaways

- **Evangelists amplify your reach** organically; design programs that make sharing effortless and rewarding.
- **Emotional loyalty** is built on purpose-driven rewards, exclusive experiences, and delightful surprises—not just discounts.
- **Community & feedback loops** turn users into collaborators, deepening their ownership and driving advocacy.

Together, these strategies transform customers into champions—driving growth, trust, and a product ecosystem that thrives on connection and shared purpose.

Up next, we'll gather real-world case studies in **Part 4**, starting with **Chapter 11: SaaS Success Stories**—where you'll see these playbooks come to life.

Ready to dive in?

Part 4: Case Studies & Real-World Examples

Chapter 11: SaaS Success Stories (My POV) — *How Others Cracked the Psychology Code*

By now, you and I have walked through the frameworks, playbooks, and strategies that help a SaaS product move from being tolerated to being truly loved.

But let's be honest—frameworks are only as good as their execution. And the real test? How companies—big and small—apply psychology to win hearts, build habits, and scale loyalty.

So in this chapter, I want to take you inside **three tiers of SaaS growth stories**:

1. Startups on their way to unicorn status.
2. Mid-size SaaS players who've nailed their niche.
3. Giants who rewrote the playbook at scale.

And as we unpack each story, I want you to pay attention to one thing:

👉 ***They didn't just understand user behavior. They shaped it.***

Startups → Unicorns: Hungry and Psychology Driven

HubSpot – Teaching Before Selling

HubSpot didn't just market software—they marketed **confidence**. Their free HubSpot Academy tapped into the **endowment effect**: once you've invested time learning, you're far less likely to walk away.

Every "Congrats—your campaign reached 500 people!" message wasn't vanity. It was psychology. It created progress, and progress keeps people hooked.

Founder Takeaway: Don't just sell features—teach, guide, and celebrate your users. People stick with what they've invested in.

CleverTap – Knowing Before You Ask

CleverTap mastered predictive personalization. Push notifications, lifecycle emails, in-app nudges—all timed so well it felt like the app "read your mind."

And when a product "gets" you, leaving feels like betrayal.

Founder Takeaway: Anticipate user needs before they voice them. Relevance isn't nice-to-have—it's loyalty insurance.

Freshworks – Growing With Users

Freshworks didn't just expand features. They expanded at the pace of their customers' growth. By solving each *new* pain point, they positioned themselves as a **partner, not a vendor**.

Founder Takeaway: Don't think "upsell." Think "evolve with your user." Products that grow with customers become irreplaceable.

Mid-Size SaaS: Building Habits, One User at a Time

Spotify – Playlists That Feel Like Magic

Spotify's genius wasn't music access. It was **identity access**. Discover Weekly felt like a gift, while collaborative playlists made music social.

That's not just streaming. That's *belonging*.

Founder Takeaway: Ask yourself: Does my product reflect my users back to themselves? Products that mirror identity become daily habits.

Duolingo – Making Learning Addictive

Streaks, badges, leaderboards—Duolingo gamified the grind. Once you've hit 30 days, your brain screams, *"Don't break the chain!"* That's commitment bias in play.

Founder Takeaway: Find the "streak" inside your product. What's the one behavior you can reward daily to build unstoppable habits?

Heap – Showing, Not Telling

Heap's marketing didn't lean on feature lists. They showcased real customer wins. When a peer claims "*We boosted conversions 5× with Heap,*" it sparks **social proof** and trust.

Founder Takeaway: Your customers are your best marketers. Capture their wins and use their stories as your strongest persuasion tool.

Enterprise SaaS: Giants Who Scale Emotions

Shopify – Belonging to a Movement

Shopify didn't just build software. They built a movement: *You're not just a user—you're a founder.*

Founder stories weren't just case studies. They were mirrors. Every entrepreneur could see themselves in the tribe.

Founder Takeaway: Elevate your customers' identity. People don't leave platforms they feel proud to belong to.

Freshworks – Humor as Differentiation

Remember "Failsforce"? The cheeky Freshworks blimp floating over Salesforce's mega-event? That wasn't just trolling. It was **personality in a sea of corporate sameness.**

Founder Takeaway: Don't be afraid of personality. In B2B SaaS, being human, funny, or bold is often the sharpest wedge against giants.

Booking.com – Trust Through Transparency

Thousands of A/B tests, openly shared. A culture where experimentation wasn't hidden but celebrated.

The user doesn't see "tests." They feel **reliability, fairness, and better options**. Trust, delivered through transparency.

Founder Takeaway: Build trust not by claiming perfection but by showing the rigor behind your decisions. Transparency creates safety—and safety drives loyalty.

The Thread That Connects Them All

So, what's the common DNA here?

- HubSpot ***educated.***
- CleverTap ***personalized.***
- Freshworks ***partnered* (and *entertained*).**
- Spotify ***connected.***
- Duolingo ***gamified.***
- Heap ***empathized.***
- Shopify ***inspired.***
- Booking.com ***built trust.***

Different levers. Same result. Emotional resonance.

Because features make people ***try***.

But emotions make people ***buy*** & ***stay***.

Well, having said all that - now it's time to see some failures and probably learn a few things from them.

Chapter 12: When Psychology Backfires — SaaS Missteps & Missed Signals

Every SaaS founder loves success stories. But let's be honest: we learn more from the **burn marks** than the **spotlights**.

Because for every HubSpot or Shopify that nailed user psychology, there are companies that ignored emotional signals, overplayed their hand, or misunderstood what truly drove behavior.

Let's look at SaaS companies across three stages—startups, mid-size, and giants—that I stumbled upon not because of bad tech, but because of **bad psychology.**

Again, the below mentioned are just my POV, something I felt that misfired.

Startups → Unicorns: Growing Too Fast, Missing the Human

Quibi – The "Nobody Asked For This" Effect

Quibi thought short-form video would explode if you threw Hollywood money at it. They ignored a basic principle: **context matters more than content.** People already had TikTok and YouTube for short videos—and those had social hooks.

Quibi had content, but no habit loop. No sharing. No identity. Result? Billions of $ lost in 6 months.

Founder Takeaway: Just because a behavior exists doesn't mean you can redirect it at will. Users adopt tools that fit their *lives*, not your pitch deck.

Zenefits – The Broken Trust Spiral

Zenefits grew fast, selling HR software, but cut compliance corners, even building hacks to bypass licensing rules. Once the truth surfaced, they weren't just seen as sloppy—they were seen as **dishonest.**

In psychology, broken trust is rarely repaired. Customers churned, regulators cracked down, and the brand collapsed.

Founder Takeaway: In SaaS, trust compounds. Break it once, and no amount of features will bring users back.

Clubhouse – Mistaking FOMO for Loyalty

Clubhouse nailed the FOMO play with invite-only exclusivity. But they mistook **curiosity spikes** for lasting engagement. Once the novelty wore off—and moderation failed—the community thinned out.

FOMO is a spark, not fuel.

Founder Takeaway: Exclusivity can create buzz, but only consistent value creates loyalty. Don't confuse noise for signal.

Mid-Size SaaS: Stalled by Misreading User Behavior

Evernote – The "Kitchen Sink" Problem

Evernote started as a beloved note-taking tool. Then they piled on features: presentation mode, chat, market stores that cluttered the user interface. Instead of delight, it caused **cognitive overload.**

Users wanted simplicity. Evernote gave them confusion. Competitors like Notion swooped in.

Founder Takeaway: `More features ≠ more love. Users bond with clarity, not clutter.`

Yammer – The Ghost Town Syndrome

Billed as the "Facebook for Work," Yammer assumed companies wanted social feeds at work. But they missed one detail: work conversations need **purpose, not noise.**

Without tight integration into workflows, Yammer became a ghost town inside companies. Microsoft eventually buried it into Microsoft Viva Engage.

Founder Takeaway: Community tools need a heartbeat. Without purpose or daily relevance, your product becomes another tab users ignore.

Rdio – Losing the "Why Me" Battle

Rdio had a beautiful design and loyal niche fans. But they failed to answer one question at scale: *Why choose us over Spotify?*

In user psychology, **clarity of value** beats elegance of design. Without differentiation, even a good product gets drowned.

Founder Takeaway: Beauty won't save you if your positioning isn't razor-sharp. Users need a reason to care, not just a reason to admire.

Enterprise SaaS: Giants That Lost Touch with Users

Salesforce – Complexity as a Churn Magnet

Salesforce is powerful, but for years, it's been infamous for being overwhelming. Many customers, plus me, feel "trapped" rather than "empowered."

The psychology miss here could be, mistaking **switching costs** for loyalty. People stay not because they love it, but because leaving is painful - it's more like an Antibiotic from the *SaaS Prescription* point of view. That resentment fuels competitors like HubSpot, Zoho, Odoo, and Pipedrive.

Founder Takeaway: Lock-in isn't love. Long-term growth comes from delight, not dependence.

Adobe (Pre-Creative Cloud) – The Sticker Shock Mistake

Before subscriptions, Adobe charged upfront for software signups. The psychology miss here could be that they ignored **price accessibility** and **commitment bias.**

People pirated Photoshop not out of malice, but because the barrier was absurd. Only when Adobe shifted to SaaS pricing did adoption actually explode, and it became a Pain Killer product from the *SaaS Prescription* point of view.

Founder Takeaway: Price isn't just economics—it's psychology. If users feel excluded, they'll find a way around you. Don't forget that Adobe alternative is still Canva.

Oracle – The Fear Play Gone Wrong

Oracle leaned heavily on aggressive sales tactics: scare customers with compliance risks, then sell "protection". From my bird's-eye view, it worked for years—but users felt bullied, not supported.

Fear-based psychology creates compliance, not advocacy. Today, Oracle fights a brand perception problem that keeps younger companies from even considering them.

Slowly, it's becoming more like a Vitamin from the *SaaS Prescription* point of view.

Founder Takeaway: Fear or FOMO can win short-term deals, but never long-term loyalty. Respect beats intimidation every time.

The Common Thread of Failure from My POV

- **Quibi, Clubhouse, Evernote:** ignored habit psychology.
- **Zenefits, Oracle, Salesforce:** broke trust or used manipulation.
- **Rdio, Yammer, Adobe:** misread value signals.

In every case, it wasn't just about the ***product***.

It was about the ***people*** using it—and the emotions totally ignored along the way.

Because in SaaS, the real killer isn't **competition**.

It's **psychology** gone wrong - yes, for real!

So, Is Your Customer Frustrated, Ignoring, or *Loving* Your Product?

If you've come this far, you already know something most SaaS founders never realize until it's too late: **building great software is not enough**.

Your product isn't just lines of code, feature releases, or dashboards.

It's an **emotional experience.**

Every click, every wait time, every unanswered support ticket, every "*aha*!" moment — it all adds up to how your users *feel* about you.

And here's the truth: in SaaS, **feelings become behavior,** and **behavior becomes revenue.** Hence, if your users can't feel you, then you will never know if your customers are frustrated, ignoring, or loving Your Product.

Frustration turns into churn. And from my experience, those customers who leave silently will ensure that your product gets hidden soon in that SaaS marketplace.

Indifference turns into ghosted or ignored trials. Beware of this segment; these guys will tell 100 others not to try your product.

Love turns into loyalty, advocacy, and growth. You need at least more than 70% of these guys in your customer base. They are your real heroes who, at times, might not give you a 5-star rating or that big 'we won because of you' testimonial. But these folks will bring another 7 folks to try your product, and who knows this better than me?

The SaaS Psychology Mindset for Continuous Growth

If you take away just one thing from this book, let it be this:

Your job as a founder, product manager, or **marketer is not just to solve problems, but to shape perceptions** and **emotions around those problems.**

That means adopting a **psychology first mindset**:

- **Curiosity over certainty.** Instead of assuming you know why users behave a certain way, you dig deeper. You observe, you test, you listen.

- **Emotion over features.** Users rarely remember the technical specs, but they always remember how you made them feel — powerful, in control, understood, valued.

- **Habits over hacks.** Sustainable growth comes not from gimmicks but from aligning your product with the rhythms of your users' daily lives.

- **Trust over tactics.** You can manipulate a user once. You can delight them for a lifetime. The compounding effect of trust is the real growth lever.

This is the mindset I think that can keep SaaS companies relevant and resilient, long after others fade.

Your Actionable Next Step: The Product Emotion Audit

Here's where you turn insight into action.

Take a few hours this week and run a **Product Emotion Audit** across your SaaS. It's simple, but powerful:

1. **List all the key touchpoints.**
   Onboarding, feature discovery, pricing page, customer support, renewal flow.

2. **Now ask one question at each touchpoint:**
   What is my user feeling here? Frustrated, ignoring, or loving?

3. **Gather signals.**

    - Frustration = high drop-offs, angry tickets, confused clicks.

    - Ignorance = trial stagnation, low engagement, ghosting.

- Love = referrals, feature adoption, unsolicited praise.

4. **Prioritize interventions.**
   Start by fixing frustration (the quickest revenue leaks). Then reignite interest among the ignored ones. Finally, double down on love by turning it into advocacy.

5. **Repeat quarterly.**
   Because emotions aren't static. They shift as your product, competition, market, and users evolve.

My Final SaaS Note

When you next open your dashboard and look at churn rates, NPS scores, or MRR growth, remember: those numbers aren't just metrics. They're mirrors of emotion.

Your users are telling you, in every action and inaction, whether they are frustrated, ignoring, or loving your product.

And now you have another SaaS prescription— not just to interpret those signals, but to act on them.

Because the future of SaaS doesn't belong to the companies with the most features, the best tech team, the largest funding rounds, or the flashiest marketing launches.

It belongs to the ones that understand — and honor — the psychology of their customers.

Now it's time - let me give you something for *Free* that you can take a printout, pin on a wall, or run through with your team.

Your Product Emotion Audit Worksheet

Frustrated, Ignoring, or Loving?

Step 1: Map Your Key Touchpoints

☐ Onboarding

☐ First use / Aha! moment

☐ Feature discovery

☐ Pricing & upgrade flow

☐ Customer support interaction

☐ Renewal / Cancellation flow

☐ Other: ____________________

Step 2: Diagnose the Emotion at Each Touchpoint

Touchpoint	User Signal	Likely Emotion	Notes
Onboarding	Drop-offs before activation	😠 Frustrated	
First Use	Trial stagnation / No return	😐 Ignoring	
Feature Use	Adoption + praise / referrals	❤️ Loving	
Pricing	Confusion / cart abandonment	😠 Frustrated	
Support	Tickets unanswered / slow	😠 Frustrated	
Renewal	Auto-churn / ghosted users	😐 Ignoring	
Community	User-generated content, word-of-mouth	❤️ Loving	

Step 3: Intervention Playbook

- **If Frustrated → Fix Leaks**

  ☐ Simplify UX flow

  ☐ Improve error handling

  ☐ Speed up support response

  ☐ Clarify pricing or onboarding

- **If Ignoring → Reignite Interest**

  ☐ Trigger re-engagement email campaigns

  ☐ Personalize in-app nudges

  ☐ Highlight relevant features & benefits

  ☐ Refresh messaging to connect emotionally

- **If Loving → Amplify the Love**

  ☐ Launch referral/advocacy programs

  ☐ Spotlight customer stories

  ☐ Build community spaces

  ☐ Create feedback loops for co-creation

Step 4: Classify Emotional Zones

Instead of traffic-light colors, use **zones of emotional connection** to categorize user sentiment:

1. **Frustration Zone → "Pain Points"**
   - Users feel blocked, confused, or stressed.
   - Signals: complaints, churn risk, support tickets piling up.
2. **Ignorance Zone → "Blind Spots"**
   - Users are disengaged, using your product minimally, or ignoring features.
   - Signals: low DAU/MAU, inactive accounts, low feature adoption.
3. **Love Zone → "Winning Moments"**
   - Users feel delighted, trust the product, and recommend it to others.

  - Signals: referrals, positive reviews, customer stories.

👉 Instead of scoring with numbers or colors, ask:

- **Which zone does this feature/experience belong to?**
- **What's one action I can take to move it to the next zone?**

☐ Completed Audit Date: ___________

☐ Next Audit Scheduled: ___________

PS: You can change this worksheet according to your needs. My objective was to let you know that there is a way to understand - is your customer frustrated, ignoring, or loving your product?

Closing the Loop - In the *End*, It's About *People*

For SaaS Founders:

You're not just building software — you're shaping human behavior. Every line of code, every pricing decision, every onboarding flow is ultimately about how someone feels when they use your product. Founders often obsess over fundraising, features, or growth hacks, but remember this: **growth is just borrowed attention; retention is earned trust.**

If you want your product to outlive trends and copycats, anchor it in user psychology. Stay close to your customers, feel their frustrations as if they were your own, and design with empathy. That's how category leaders are born.

For SaaS Product Managers:

Your job is not feature delivery. Your job is emotional orchestration. A roadmap full of "things to ship" is worthless if those things don't reduce friction, build trust, or spark joy for users. As a PM, you're the bridge between what users need and what your company builds. Carry that responsibility with pride.

Constantly ask yourself: *Does this make my user feel smarter, more confident, more capable? Or does it burden them with more complexity?*

Products live and die not by the features they launch, but by the feelings they leave behind.

For SaaS Product Marketers:

You are the voice in the user's head before they even click "sign up." Messaging isn't copywriting — it's psychology in motion. If you market a product that frustrates, you're fueling churn. If you market with indifference, you'll be ignored. But when you market with empathy — speaking to pain, aspiration, and transformation — you create resonance. Your role is to turn customer love into stories, advocacy, and momentum.

Remember: **features inform, but emotions persuade.** Make your messaging not about what your product *does*, but how it makes your users *feel*.

My Top 21 Must-Reads List

If this book has sparked your curiosity about the intersection of **psychology, behavior, product marketing, and product management**, here are twenty-one powerful books I personally recommend. Each one has shaped how I think about *customers*, *products*, and *growth*.

◇ Consumer Psychology & Behavior

1. **Influence: The Psychology of Persuasion** – Robert Cialdini
   Why read: The ultimate playbook on the six principles of persuasion every marketer and product leader should master.

2. **Predictably Irrational** – Dan Ariely
   Why read: Explains why customers don't always act rationally—and how you can design around it.

3. **Thinking, Fast and Slow** – Daniel Kahneman
   Why read: A deep dive into how humans make decisions, blending intuition (fast) with reasoning (slow).

4. **Hooked: How to Build Habit-Forming Products** – Nir Eyal
   Why read: A practical framework for creating products users keep coming back to.

5. **The Paradox of Choice** – Barry Schwartz
   Why read: Shows how too many options can overwhelm users—and how simplifying can drive adoption.

- **Product Marketing**

6. **Obviously Awesome** – April Dunford
   Why read: The definitive guide to positioning your product so customers instantly "get it."

7. **Crossing the Chasm** – Geoffrey A. Moore
   Why read: Explains how tech products move from early adopters to the mainstream.

8. **Made to Stick** – Chip Heath & Dan Heath
   Why read: Reveals why some ideas thrive while others fade—and how to craft sticky messages.

9. **Building a StoryBrand** – Donald Miller
   Why read: Helps you simplify your brand's message so

customers listen.

10. **Influenced: The Psychology of Marketing That Actually Works** – Robert Cialdini
    Why read: A practical extension of *Influence*, applied directly to modern marketing.

Product Management

11. **Inspired: How to Create Tech Products Customers Love** – Marty Cagan
    Why read: A must-read bible for anyone building software products that win markets.

12. **Empowered: Ordinary People, Extraordinary Products** – Marty Cagan & Chris Jones
    Why read: Teaches how to build empowered product teams that consistently innovate.

13. **The Lean Product Playbook** – Dan Olsen
    Why read: A step-by-step process for applying Lean principles to product development.

14. **Escaping the Build Trap** – Melissa Perri
    Why read: Explains why building more features doesn't

always mean delivering more value.

15. **Continuous Discovery Habits** – Teresa Torres
Why read: Practical tools for running continuous user research and making customer-informed decisions.

◇ Bridging Psychology + Product Strategy

16. **The Mom Test** – Rob Fitzpatrick
Why read: Teaches how to ask customers the right questions—so they tell you the truth.

17. **Start with Why** – Simon Sinek
Why read: A powerful reminder that customers don't just buy what you do—they buy *why* you do it.

18. **The Design of Everyday Things** – Don Norman
Why read: A timeless classic on how design influences usability and human behavior.

19. **Contagious: Why Things Catch On** – Jonah Berger
Why read: Shows why certain products and ideas go viral—and how to engineer shareability.

20. **Drive: The Surprising Truth About What Motivates Us** – Daniel H. Pink
 Why read: Breaks down what truly motivates people—and how you can apply it to product engagement.

👉 This list definitely blends **timeless classics** with **modern playbooks** — giving you both the *why* (human psychology and behavior) and the *how* (practical frameworks for product and marketing).

FYI, all books are available on Amazon.com

21. The SaaS Prescription: Is Your Product a Painkiller, Antibiotic, or *Vitamin*? – *Aries Ram*

Before I wrote ***The SaaS Psychology***, I published my very first book: ***The SaaS Prescription***.

This one is special to me because it was the starting point of my journey as an author.

In it, I did break down a simple but powerful framework that asks a question every SaaS founder, product manager and product marketer wrestles with: *Is your product a Painkiller, an Antibiotic, or just a Vitamin?*

Understanding where your product fits in this spectrum can completely change how you build it, position it, message it, market it, and scale it.

If *The SaaS Psychology* helps you understand how your customers **feel** about your product, *The SaaS Prescription* helps you understand how to **position** your product so those feelings turn into adoption, loyalty, and growth.

If you haven't read it yet, I'd love for you to check out a sample read of it on *Amazon*—it's where this whole journey started for me. Please scan the QR code below to find the book!

SCAN HERE

Thank you "__________" for reading **The SaaS Psychology: Is Your Customer Frustrated, Ignoring, or Loving Your Product?** – truly, I mean that.

Writing this book was a conversation I wanted to have with real product people: founders juggling roadmaps, marketers hunting for one message that actually sticks, and Product Managers who quietly carry the weight of customer experience.

If anything in these pages landed for you – a phrase, a question, a tactic – it was worth writing. If something didn't land, I want to hear that too. Honest feedback is how better work gets made.

Please do two small things that will make a big dent in this universe: **run the Product Emotion Audit inside** (it's short, actionable, and built to surface exactly what your users are feeling-you can even edit it according to your thoughts/world view).

And **if this book helped**, please leave a quick brutally honest review where you bought it. Reviews help other busy practitioners find tools that actually work.

Plus if you try one of the playbooks, I'd love to know what changed – small wins are worth celebrating.

This is one stop on a longer journey.

If you read my first book, ***The SaaS Prescription***, you know I'm obsessed with helping teams be clearer about the value they deliver.

So, this book is the next step: turn feeling into action.

Thank you for investing your time.

Now go find the friction, plug the leaks, and create a product people can't imagine working without and would proudly tell others about naturally.

With gratitude,

Aries Ram

The SaaS Psychology: **Is Your Customer** *Frustrated*, **Ignoring**, or Loving **Your Product**?

by **Aries Ram**

Disclaimer

The information provided in this book is based on the author's experience, research, and observations in the field of SaaS product marketing and management. It is intended solely for educational and informational purposes. While every effort has been made to ensure accuracy, the author and publisher make no representations or warranties with respect to the completeness, reliability, or applicability of the content provided.

This book does not constitute professional advice, nor should it be relied upon as such. Readers are encouraged to seek appropriate professional guidance for their specific business, legal, or financial circumstances. The author and publisher disclaim any liability for any loss, risk, or damages, personal or otherwise, incurred directly or indirectly as a result of the use and application of any of the contents of this book.

All case studies, company references, and examples included in this book are either publicly available, adapted for educational purposes, or represent the author's interpretations. Unless explicitly stated, the author is not affiliated with, sponsored by, or endorsed by any of the companies mentioned.

Copyright

The SaaS Psychology: Is Your Customer Frustrated, Ignoring, or Loving Your Product?